Cornerstones of Freedom

Tecumseh

Zachary Kent

CP CHILDRENS PRESS ®
CHICAGO

Library of Congress Cataloging-in-Publication Data

Kent, Zachary.
Tecumseh / by Zachary Kent.
    p. cm. — (Cornerstones of freedom)
  Summary: A biography of the Shawnee warrior, orator,
and leader who united a confederacy of Indians in an
effort to save Indian land from the advance of white
soldiers and settlers.
  ISBN 0-516-06660-9
  1. Tecumseh, Shawnee Chief, 1768-1813—Juvenile
literature. 2. Shawnee Indians—Biography—Juvenile
literature. 3. Shawnee Indians—History—Juvenile
literature. [1. Tecumseh, Shawnee Chief, 1768-1813
2. Shawnee Indians—Biography. 3. Indians of North
America—Biography.] I. Title. II. Series.
E99.S35T162   1992
973.04973—dc20
                                    92-8217
                                      CIP
                                      AC

Excitement gripped the Creek Indians as they waited in their village on a September night in 1811. Young warriors pounded drums and shook gourd instruments. Older chiefs chanted in loud voices and stared at the flickering flames of the council fire.

Suddenly, the people fell quiet as a man stepped forward out of the darkness. This tall, dignified man wore unadorned buckskin and a silver bracelet around each arm. His head was shaven except for a single braid of black hair intertwined with hawk feathers that hung down his back. Beneath each of his deep, hazel eyes, a slash of red war paint marked his face. The Creek gazed with respect at the famous Shawnee chief Tecumseh.

Every year, American settlers had been pushing farther westward, grabbing up lands that Indians had lived on for centuries. Tecumseh had a plan to save the Indian homelands. He traveled north and south, from the Great Lakes to the Gulf of Mexico, calling upon the various Indian tribes to join together to form a united Indian nation.

The great Shawnee chief Tecumseh

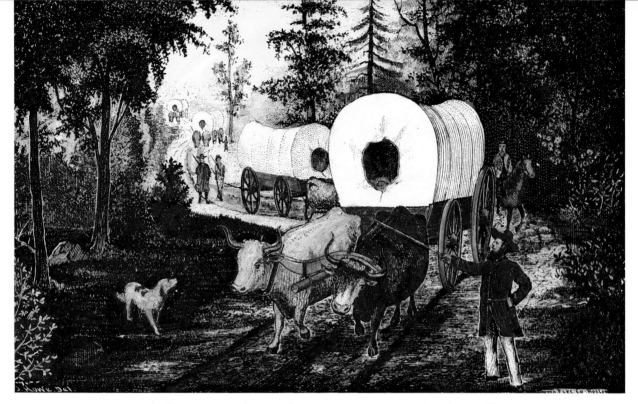

By the late 1700s, white settlers were moving into the Ohio Valley.

Working together, he thought, they might be strong enough to hold off the waves of white settlers. But Tecumseh's ultimate goal was peace, not war. His dream was to create a great Indian country that would stretch from Canada to the Gulf of Mexico and exist as a peaceful neighbor to the United States. It was becoming clear to Tecumseh that to achieve this dream, a united military stand would be necessary. That is why he stood before this gathering of Creek in the Alabama wilderness.

"Where today are the Pequot?" Tecumseh cried out to his listeners. "Where are the Narragansett, the Mohican, the Pokanoket and many other once powerful tribes of our people? They have vanished before the avarice and oppression of the white man, as snow before a summer sun. . . . Will we let ourselves be destroyed in our turn without making an effort worthy of our race? Shall we, without a struggle, give up our homes, our country . . . and everything that is dear and sacred to us? I know you will cry with me, Never! Never!"

Many of the Creek warriors shouted their approval. If anyone could unite the Indians against their common foe, surely it would be this proud Shawnee, Tecumseh.

The Shawnee had long been known as a strong, independent people. It was their custom in the winter to cross the Ohio River Valley, hunting deer and elk. During the warmer

Indians camping along the Wabash River in the early 1800s

months, they camped in villages along the Little Miami River and planted corn and other crops.

Sometime around 1768, near present-day Springfield, Ohio, the wife of a Shawnee chief gave birth to a baby boy. Village chiefs later named him *Tecumseh*, meaning "Crouching Panther" or "Shooting Star."

Growing up, Tecumseh wrestled playfully with his older brothers and rambled through the woods learning hunting skills. At night, around the village campfires, he listened carefully as the older Shawnee men told proud stories of their people's history and culture.

As early as the 1760s, white men threatened the Shawnee way of life. The sound of axes rang

During Tecumseh's childhood, white settlers began clearing farms and building forts on land that the Shawnee had lived on for centuries.

Indians raiding an Ohio River flatboat in the late 1700s

through the wilderness as pioneers built forts and cleared farms. The Shawnee resisted the advance of the settlers into the Ohio River Valley, and Tecumseh's father died in one early battle. As the struggle continued into the 1780s, young Tecumseh took his place among the Shawnee warriors, conducting raids on river flatboats and settlers' cabins.

In 1793, President George Washington ordered protection for American settlements. Cavalry horses snorted and artillery wheels rumbled as an American army of three thousand men commanded by Major General Anthony Wayne slowly advanced northward. On August 20, 1794,

Anthony Wayne

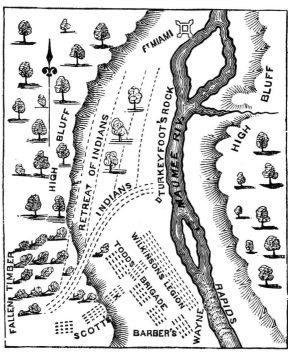

Tecumseh was among those who fought against the forces of General "Mad" Anthony Wayne in the 1794 Battle of Fallen Timbers.

they reached a place beside the Maumee River, near present-day Toledo, Ohio, where a tornado had knocked down hundreds of trees. Here, at "Fallen Timbers," Shawnee chief Blue Jacket waited with a force of thirteen hundred allied Indians.

The Indians fired musket volleys and sent arrows whizzing as the Americans attacked. "Charge the damned rascals with the bayonet," yelled General Wayne. The thrusting bayonets proved too much for the outnumbered Indians. "We ran to the river, swamps, thickets, and to the islands in the river," Ottawa chief Kinjoino later exclaimed. Though Tecumseh fought bravely in this battle, he soon joined the Indian retreat.

A year after the crushing defeat at Fallen
Timbers, ninety-two chiefs representing twelve
different Indian nations signed the Treaty of
Greenville. Under this agreement, the Indians
surrendered most of central and southern Ohio
to the United States. In return, they were paid
$20,000 in goods and were promised another
$9,500 in yearly payments. Tecumseh, however,
took no part in the peace council at Greenville.
He refused to sign a treaty that gave away huge
tracts of tribal land in exchange for some blankets
and a few kegs of rum. He knew that nothing,
certainly not the sum of money that was offered,
could pay for the loss of those lands. With a band
of loyal Shawnee followers, he journeyed
westward and settled along the White River in
Indiana.

During the next few years of uneasy peace,
Tecumseh occasionally returned to Ohio to hunt
and trade. Whenever Tecumseh entered a white
settlement, the people stared at the tall,
handsome, young Shawnee chief and noticed the
look of authority in his intent hazel eyes.

Often, Tecumseh observed white traders selling
whiskey to the Indians. In many places, he saw
Indians dying of diseases that had been brought
to North America by white settlers. He watched
settlers cut down forests to make farmland, and
soon learned that General William Henry
Harrison, U.S. governor of the Indiana Territory,

Tenskwatawa, Tecumseh's brother, became a famous spiritual leader.

was arranging treaties to take even more land from the Indians. Tecumseh vowed to stop the further ruin of his people.

By chance, Tecumseh's younger brother, Lalawethika, helped him in his efforts. Lalawethika grew up overshadowed by his older brother. As a boy, he had been blinded in one eye in an accident with an arrow. Whereas Tecumseh was a great hunter and athlete, Lalawethika seemed hopelessly lazy. As an adult, he became addicted to alcohol. The people of his village considered him a lost cause.

One night in April 1805, after a heavy bout of drinking, Lalawethika collapsed in his cabin and fell into a deep stupor. His wife and friends believed he was dead. The next day, however, he stirred and slowly regained his senses. He claimed that during his trance, he had met the

*Tenskwatawa
preaching
to followers*

supreme Master of Life, who revealed to him
how to save the Indians from doom. They must
give up liquor and other white men's customs
and return completely to their traditional way of
life. Overnight, Lalawethika became a changed
man. He never drank again. People from many
different tribes, including the Kickapoo, Ottawa,
Potawatomi, and Winnebago, traveled great
distances to hear him describe his mystical
visions. With renewed pride, they gave up
drinking whiskey and threw off their white men's
clothes. To show he had become a new man,
Lalawethika changed his name to *Tenskwatawa,*
meaning "The Open Door" or "I Am the Door." As
his fame spread, he became known as the Prophet.

Tenskwatawa attempts to convince Governor Harrison of his powers.

Governor Harrison attempted to stop the Prophet's growing influence. In April 1806, Harrison challenged Tenskwatawa to perform a miracle. "If he is really a prophet," Harrison declared, "ask him to cause the sun to stand still, the moon to alter its course, the rivers to cease to flow, or the dead to rise from their graves."

The Prophet accepted Harrison's challenge. On June 16, 1806, a huge crowd of Indians gathered at the Shawnee settlement at Greenville, Ohio. The Prophet walked among them and, pointing at the sky, asked the Great Spirit to blacken the sun. Sure enough, at 11:32 A.M., the moon crossed before the sun and temporarily turned day into night. The Indians who witnessed this miracle were awestruck. They did not guess that

Tenskwatawa had learned in advance, perhaps from some white man with an almanac, that there would be a total solar eclipse that day.

Word of the Prophet's power spread like wildfire across the region. Tecumseh and his brother soon established a new village, called Prophetstown, along the banks of Tippecanoe Creek in Indiana. When not welcoming visitors there, they traveled far and wide, seeking Indian followers. Governor Harrison was disturbed by the growing unrest among the Indians. In 1810, he invited the Prophet to come to Vincennes, the settlement along the Wabash River that served as the capital of the Indiana Territory. Tecumseh decided that he would go in his brother's place.

United States soldiers at Vincennes stared in wonder when Tecumseh arrived on August 12. Eighty canoes landed at the riverside, and some four hundred Indians stepped ashore. One anxious army captain noted that the Indians "were all painted in the most terrific manner . . . and well prepared for war."

The Indians encamped near the governor's mansion, and two days later, the meetings began outdoors underneath the trees. Tecumseh spoke first, reminding Harrison of the many unfair things the whites had done to the Indians since entering the Ohio River Valley. "The way, the only way to stop this evil," the Shawnee chief exclaimed, "is for all the red men to unite in claiming . . . the land." Those chiefs who had signed away land in treaties, Tecumseh declared loudly, had no right to do so. "Sell a country! Why not sell the air, the clouds and the great sea, as well as the earth? Did not the Great Spirit make them all for the use of his children?" At the end of this eloquent speech, the Shawnee leader defiantly sat on the ground rather than sit in the chair offered by Harrison.

The tension mounted as Harrison responded. He insisted sternly that the United States had always dealt fairly with the Indians. "It is false! He lies!" shouted Tecumseh, jumping angrily to his feet. Defensively, Harrison drew his sword. In an instant, nearby officers cocked their pistols and Indians pulled tomahawks from their belts. Before fighting could break out, Harrison coolly ordered that the council adjourn for the day.

The next day, Tecumseh apologized for his outburst. As legend has it, he then, in a more cheerful mood, sat beside Governor Harrison on a wooden bench. As they talked, Tecumseh kept moving closer to Harrison, forcing the governor to shift. Finally, as he was about to be shoved off the bench, Harrison complained. With a laugh, Tecumseh pointed out that he was only doing to Harrison what the American settlers were doing to the Indians.

A few days later, Tecumseh and his followers left Vincennes, having gained nothing. The

A tense moment during Tecumseh's meeting with William Henry Harrison at Vincennes in 1810

Shawnee chief had not been able to persuade Harrison to give back the treaty lands. That fall, Tecumseh continued his bold efforts to unite the various Indian tribes. He hurried through Ohio, Indiana, Michigan, Illinois, and Wisconsin, delivering emotional speeches at every Indian village he visited. His message reached the Winnebago, Menominee, Kickapoo, Miami, Delaware, and Potawatomi, and even the Ottawa Indians of Canada. In August 1811, Tecumseh and twenty-one of his closest followers began a five-month journey into the South in search of support. It was the tireless Shawnee leader's greatest effort yet. His forceful speeches shook

Tecumseh and his followers arriving at an Indian council

the hearts and minds of Osage warriors in Missouri, Chickasaw in Mississippi, Creek in Alabama, Choctaw in Georgia, and Seminole in Florida.

At each village, Tecumseh and his followers arrived riding handsome, jet-black horses. Always they dressed proudly in simple, traditional Indian clothing. Whenever Tecumseh spoke, he wore bright slashes of war paint on his face. None who saw him ever forgot it. His words "fell in avalanches from his lips," one listener later declared, "his eyes burned with supernatural lustre, and his whole frame trembled with emotion." Time and time again, the Shawnee leader stood alone and made his plea for help and unity.

"For four years, he has been in constant motion," General Harrison warned the United States War Department. "You see him today on the Wabash, and in a short time hear of him on the shores of Lake Erie or Michigan, or on the banks of the Mississippi; and wherever he goes, he makes an impression favorable to his purposes."

Harrison decided to act before Tecumseh gathered an army of Indians too powerful to beat. In the fall of 1811, soon after Tecumseh had left for the South, Harrison began preparations to destroy Prophetstown. He reasoned that it would be better to crush the Indian settlement while Tecumseh was away, rather than wait until the Shawnee chief returned, perhaps with more warriors than before.

Harrison marched one thousand militiamen up the Wabash River. On November 6, the American soldiers camped a few miles from Tippecanoe Creek. In Prophetstown, the Indians held a council. Although they wished to avoid a fight if possible, they were not afraid of one. After much discussion, they decided it was best to attack before the army attacked them. The Prophet had less than five hundred warriors at Prophetstown. Even so, he predicted confidently that the Great Spirit would protect the Indians in battle. He

William Henry Harrison

A map of General Harrison's march to Tippecanoe

17

The Indian defeat at Tippecanoe was a setback for Tecumseh's efforts.

promised that nothing could hurt the warriors, and urged them to attack.

The Indians charged the American camp at dawn on November 7, 1811. Terrified soldiers jumped from their blankets and grabbed their muskets. Bullets whistled through the trees and gunsmoke soon choked the air. Desperately, the whites beat back the first charge of the Indians. The Indians courageously charged the camp again until dozens of Indians and whites lay dead and wounded. At last, however, as the sun rose, the outnumbered, bloodied Indians retreated. Before returning to Vincennes, Harrison's army burned Prophetstown to the ground.

Left: Tecumseh, furious, berates Tenskwatawa for letting the Indians attack Harrison's forces at Tippecanoe
Right: President Madison's offical statement about the battle

The Indian defeat at Tippecanoe destroyed the myth of the Prophet's power and was a serious setback for Tecumseh's efforts. When Tecumseh arrived back in Indiana, he angrily sent his brother into exile.

Now Tecumseh grasped at one last hope of saving the Indian homelands. On June 18, 1812, after years of arguments and clashes, the United States declared war against Great Britain. "Here is a chance . . ." exclaimed Tecumseh, "yes, a chance such as will never occur again—for us

British general Isaac Brock (right) gave Tecumseh a compass (above) just before the two leaders attacked Detroit.

Indians of North America to form ourselves into one great combination." He quickly chose to join the British colonists of Canada in fighting the Americans in the War of 1812. He reasoned that if Great Britain won the war, the Indians, as British allies, could demand land for a separate Indian nation as part of the peace treaty.

The British, recognizing Tecumseh's leadership abilities, made him a brigadier general in command of Indian allies. Immediately, Tecumseh set about assembling what was probably the most impressive force ever commanded by a North American Indian. Indian messengers ran along the trails leading north,

20

A view of Amherstburg, Ontario, in 1813

south, and west. Bands of warriors heard Tecumseh's call and joined the fight. Parties of Wyandot, Chippewa, Sioux, Sauk, Fox, and Winnebago soon entered Tecumseh's camp ready for battle.

Twice during the first days of August 1812, Tecumseh and his men successfully ambushed columns of American troops along the Michigan-Canada border. The sound of Indian yells and the crack of rifle fire sent hundreds of soldiers running. Still, Tecumseh longed for even greater victories. At Amherstburg, in Ontario, Canada, he met with British general Isaac Brock. Together, the two leaders decided to attack nearby Detroit, the strongest American fort in the Northwest.

General Hull surrenders Detroit to General Brock and Tecumseh.

The mixed force of about six hundred British troops and seven hundred Indian warriors reached the outskirts of Detroit on August 15. Immediately, Brock sent a message into the fort demanding that General William Hull and his fifteen hundred soldiers surrender. When Hull refused, Brock gave a signal, and six light cannon roared, sending British cannonballs crashing over the fort's high wooden walls.

Soon a white flag fluttered over the fort. General Hull surrendered without a struggle. Side by side, General Brock and Tecumseh rode into Detroit on August 16. It was a moment of great triumph for the Shawnee chief.

Throughout the fall and winter, Tecumseh kept British-allied Indians fighting throughout the American Northwest. Potawatomi warriors captured Fort Dearborn (present-day Chicago). In the South, Creek warriors answered Tecumseh's call by attacking Alabama settlements. In April 1813, Tecumseh returned to Amherstburg, only to learn that his friend General Brock had died in battle. Now General Henry Procter commanded the British in the Great Lakes region.

Tecumseh and Procter agreed to work together. Tecumseh's old enemy William Henry Harrison

Answering Tecumseh's call, Potawatomi warriors attacked Fort Dearborn in present-day Illinois.

After stopping some warriors who were murdering captured American soldiers (left), Tecumseh reprimanded General Procter (right) for allowing men under his command to behave so cruelly.

commanded twelve hundred American soldiers stationed at Fort Meigs on the Maumee River. On April 25, 1813, Harrison gazed through his spyglass and saw that his fort was surrounded by Indians and redcoats. Ten days later, Tecumseh's warriors attacked an approaching relief column of eleven hundred Kentuckians with such fury that they killed a hundred of the whites and captured another five hundred.

Tecumseh quickly lost his respect for General Procter, however, when the Englishman allowed some drunken Indians to murder prisoners. Tecumseh had long been known as someone who would not tolerate the mistreatment of prisoners. At the age of sixteen, while participating in a raid, he had seen Indians burn a white prisoner at the stake. He was so horrified by the sight that when he became a chief, he never allowed his men to torture prisoners or treat them unfairly. "You are unfit to command," Tecumseh is said to have shouted at Procter after stopping the cruel massacre. "Go and put on petticoats."

The siege of Fort Meigs continued, but the stubborn Americans refused to surrender. Finally, the frustrated Indians and British returned across the Detroit River to Amherstburg to make

The siege of Fort Meigs

General Procter ordered his men to retreat after hearing that Oliver H. Perry had won a decisive battle on Lake Erie (above).

further plans. On September 14, 1813, Tecumseh awakened to find the British hurrying eastward in full retreat. The day before, U.S. commodore Oliver Hazard Perry had won a great naval victory on Lake Erie. Now the American fleet threatened to cut off Procter's men from their eastern Canadian supply bases. Breathless Indian scouts also warned that General Harrison had crossed the Detroit River and was marching into Canada with a new army of three thousand men. Reluctantly, Tecumseh realized that he had no choice but to join the fleeing British. He and his men bravely assumed the responsibility of covering the British force's retreat.

Tecumseh and six hundred loyal warriors caught up with General Procter's British army of six hundred men near the Canadian settlement of Moraviantown on October 4. Arguing bitterly with the British general, Tecumseh persuaded him to make a stand against the advancing Americans. Beside the Thames River, the British soldiers wheeled their artillery into position, facing westward down the road. Farther to the north, Tecumseh placed his warriors along a low ridge between two swamps.

That night, Tecumseh sat gravely before a crackling campfire with his closest followers beside him. The Shawnee leader felt no real hope

A plan of the 1813 Battle of the Thames

A belt owned by Tecumseh

for success with the British the next day. "The Americans will brush them all away, like chaff before the wind," he predicted quietly. Gazing into the fire, he also guessed at his own future. "Brother warriors," he remarked calmly, "we are about to enter an engagement from which I shall not return. My body will remain on the field of battle."

On the afternoon of October 5, 1813, blaring bugles and steady drumbeats announced the approaching American army. Spurring their horses, one thousand Kentucky cavalrymen led the charge into the British line. The stunned redcoats fired a single volley before they were overwhelmed. General Procter whipped up the horses of his carriage and fled the field as most of his troops threw up their hands in surrender.

Turning northward, General Harrison next ordered his army to attack Tecumseh's Indian forces in the swampland. The Americans charged through the muddy thickets and undergrowth and fought the Indians in bloody hand-to-hand combat. Moving everywhere along the line, Tecumseh shouted encouragement to his warriors. "Be brave! Be brave!" Tecumseh yelled, and the Indians fought furiously. Then, suddenly, the Shawnee chief's voice was heard no more. Some Indians later claimed they saw Tecumseh fall. According to one account, he was standing over a wounded American officer, with his

This fictionalized depiction of the death of Tecumseh was meant to promote Richard Johnson's campaign for vice-president by portraying him as the person who slayed the Shawnee leader.

tomahawk raised, when the man shot him with a pistol. After the fighting, however, no one could find Tecumseh's body.

Soon the swamp fell silent. Without their leader to inspire them, the Indians at the Battle of the Thames quickly scattered in total defeat. In fact, word of Tecumseh's death ended serious resistance by the Indians throughout the entire American Northwest. The dream of a united Indian nation died with the Shawnee leader.

HARRISON VICTORIOUS:

Copy of a letter from General HARRISON to the Department of War....Head-Quarters, near Moravian Town, on the River Thames, 80 miles from Detroit, 5th October, 1813.

SIR---I have the honor to inform you, that by the blessing of Providence, the army under my command has this evening obtained a complete victory over the combined British and Indian forces, under the command of General Proctor. I believe that nearly the whole of the enemy's regulars are taken or killed. Amongst the former are all the superior officers ex cepting General Proctor. My mounted men are now in pursuit of him Our loss is very trifling. The brave Col. R. M. Johnson is the only officer whom I have heard of that is wounded, he badly, but I hope not dangerously. I have the honor to be with great respect, Sir, your obedient humble servant, WM. H. HARRISON.

The Hon. JOHN ARMSTRONG, Secretary at War.

LET Britons and Indians in battle combine,
Let e'en all the forces of Satan them join,
Columbians their power most boldly defy.
And for Freedom they boldly will conquer or die.
    CHORUS.
Brave Harrison's army, victorious have prov'd,
And from tyrants have rescu'd the land which they lov'd.

While PERRY most bravely Lake Erie has snapt,
And at once into victory's arms boldly leap'd,
Bold *Harrison* quick follow'd up in the game.
And has reap'd his full share of the laurels of fame.
    Brave Harrison's army, victorious have prov'd,
    And from tyrants have rescu'd the land which they lov'd.

John Bull has long vaunted, by land and by sea,
That equal to him, there no other could be ;
For he thought 'cause the *Monsieur*, he flogg'd on the wave,
He would send the whole universe down to the grave.
    Brave Harrison's army, victorious have prov'd,
    And from tyrants have rescu'd the land which they lov'd.

But John has most surely found out to his cost,
That for once he has reckon'd forgetting the host,
And long the *old fellow* will rue the sad day,
He sent *Proctor* to have with a Yankee, the fray.
    Brave Harrison's army, victorious have prov'd,
    And from tyrants have rescu'd the land which they lov'd;

Within the next twenty years, most of Tecumseh's defeated Indian allies had surrendered their homelands and trudged westward to reservations across the Mississippi River.

Friends of Colonel Richard Johnson declared that Johnson had been the officer who killed Tecumseh. Winning national fame as the "Hero of the Thames," Johnson served as vice-president of the United States from 1837 to 1841. American voters remembered General William Henry Harrison, as well. They put "Old Tippecanoe" in the White House as ninth president of the United States after the election of 1840.

Yet even in death, Tecumseh overshadowed his conquerers. Throughout the United States, people marveled at the thrilling life and legend of

One artist's conception of how Tecumseh might have looked

the noble Shawnee leader. His heartfelt speeches had brought the Indians together in a common cause, and in war, he had fought heroically, defending the rights of his people.

In 1820, an American newspaper, the *Indiana Sentinel*, perhaps described the Shawnee leader best: "Every schoolboy in the Union now knows that Tecumseh was a great man. He was truly great—and his greatness was his own. . . . As a statesman, a warrior and a patriot, take him all in all, we shall not look upon his like again."

INDEX

PHOTO CREDITS

Cover, Historical Pictures/Stock Montage; 1, Ohio Historical Society; 2, The Bettmann Archive; 3, Greene County Historical Society; 4, 5, 6 (left), North Wind; 6 (right), The Bettmann Archive; 7 (top), Historical Pictures/Stock Montage; 7 (bottom), North Wind; 8 (left), Ohio Historical Society; 8 (right), North Wind; 10, Historical Pictures/Stock Montage; 11, 12, North Wind; 15, 16, 17 (both photos), 18, Historical Pictures/Stock Montage; 19 (left), North Wind; 19 (right), Historical Pictures/Stock Montage; 20 (left), Courtesy of the Royal Ontario Museum, Toronto, Canada; 20 (right), North Wind; 21, Environment Canada, Parks Service, Fort Malden National Historic Site; 22, 23, 24 (left), Historical Pictures/Stock Montage; 24 (right), 25, The Bettmann Archive; 26, Archives of '76; 27, North Wind; 28, Environment Canada, Parks Service, Fort Malden National Historic Site; 29, The Bettmann Archive; 30, Historical Pictures/Stock Montage; 31, Field Museum of Natural History (Neg #A-93851.1ᶜ), Chicago

Picture Identifications
Cover: A portrait of Tecumseh
Page 1: Tecumseh meeting with William Henry Harrison at Vincennes
Page 2: A nineteenth-century engraving of an Indian council fire

Project Editor: Shari Joffe
Designer: Karen Yops
Cornerstones of Freedom Logo: David Cunningham

ABOUT THE AUTHOR

Zachary Kent grew up in Little Falls, New Jersey, and received a degree in English from St. Lawrence University. After college, he worked at a New York City literary agency for two years and then launched his writing career. Mr. Kent has had a lifelong interest in American history. Studying the United States presidents was his childhood hobby.